J. H Potter

Across the Continent and Back Again

J. H Potter

Across the Continent and Back Again

ISBN/EAN: 9783744686105

Printed in Europe, USA, Canada, Australia, Japan

Cover: Foto ©Thomas Meinert / pixelio.de

More available books at **www.hansebooks.com**

ACROSS THE CONTINENT

AND BACK AGAIN.

BY

REV. J. H. POTTER,

EUSTIS, FLA.

CINCINNATI, O.:

Elm Street Printing Co., Nos. 176 and 178 Elm St.

1893.

TO THE READER.

The publication of these letters in *The Presbyterian Banner* was at the earnest request of friends. It has been gratifying to learn from many sources that they have been read with interest; and they now appear in this form at the solicitation of those who wish them preserved in more permanent form. They grew from items picked up, and thoughts suggested, while on the wing.

J. H. P.

ACROSS THE CONTINENT AND BACK AGAIN.

BY REV. J. H. POTTER, OF EUSTIS, FLA.

A trip of over nine thousand miles, across the Western continent from southeast to northwest and back again, was to me one of pleasure, and has left pictures of joy in the gallery of memory. I shall be pleased to have my friends share the enjoyment with me.

I left Eustis, Florida, 160 miles south of Jacksonville, on the 29th of April, 1892, and traveled *via* Jacksonville and Tallahassee, taking in North Florida, which is so greatly different from South Florida as to be of much interest to one from the land of oranges coming to this country of grain and farm land, deciduous trees, and slow-going people.

NEW ORLEANS.

Through Mobile and Pensacola we came on to New Orleans. The old portion of that city presents nothing very attractive except to those that enjoy studying the past in the records it has left in the narrow streets and antique architecture of the old French quarters. I was pleased in visiting the new part of this old city. Long avenues, lined on both sides with stately magnolias clad in their royal robes of beauty, decorated as they then were with such flowers as none but the magnolia produce, gave the streets an attractive appearance. The lawns and the roses in wondrous profusion added greatly to the scene, and in the middle of the avenue were two rows of beauteous trees, the space between being covered with a green sward, on which the street railway track was laid, over which our cars ran free from dust. The city, taken as a whole, is perhaps not growing, but many are removing from the older to the newer portion of the city. The city lies below the level of the great river on whose banks it is located. It is called the Crescent City, as is well known, from the fact of the river flowing like a crescent in great part around it till on the west it flows from south to north. The " Father of Waters" holds his rod in his hand, and ofttimes keeps his children living on his banks in dread. Ceaseless vigilance is the price of safety. It is a high-water tax they are obliged to pay continually. All property is subject to this necessary rent. It never can be paid off so as to own the property in fee simple. Every great rise in the river demands attention. As we left the city we saw water-lines on many tenements, some six or seven feet from the ground, where the last high-water had marked its domain.

From this city we took the through train for California, and glided pleasantly on in a Pullman car by sugar-cane plantations in Louisiana.

TEXAS.

We woke up in Texas to be greeted by the far-reaching prairies, beautifully green with pastures for Texas ponies and cattle. Clumps of timber here and there break the monotony of the picture. We now approach Houston, whose aspiring steeples and massive towers proclaim it a city of taste and enterprise. It brings up memories of the long ago when Sam Houston figured in the early history of the State. I can readily believe Rev. Daniel Baker's account of his weary wanderings in his own track on these seemingly boundless prairies. The world does move. Texas has made amazing progress since it was redeemed from Mexican thraldom, and "our boys" went with musket in hand to establish *our* claim to this beautiful land. It did seem as though "might made right," and we possessed Texas, and California was taken to pay the expenses of the war. Then followed '49 and the golden era, and the star of empire moved west. In all these movements the Providence is visible pointing forward. As we glided on across the enchanting prairies of Texas that seem practically limitless, the cattle grazing, ponies feeding, sun shining, fleecy clouds floating leisurely by as chariots of God, with good angels lingering to take some message to heaven, it was manifest that He who spake in parables on earth is so speaking yet, illustrating great truths of his nature and government. By and by we pass through the city of San Antonio, said to contain some forty-five thousand inhabitants. Four cities in Texas claim pre-eminence—Houston, San Antonio, Dallas and Galveston. They are said to be of about equal size. Surely Texas has vast possibilities. In extent it is an empire equal to France. Its fertile soil and genial climate make it attractive. I slept, and woke up next morning in Western Texas, which presents a very different picture from that of Eastern and Central Texas. It abounds in arid foot hills, rainless and barren, barely enough grass to starve a few specimens of cattle that dared attempt to live so far away. Some timid antelopes were trying to feed their scant bodies on the spare tufts of grass. Shy creatures! I do not see how the Chicagoans are going to catch them to grace the World's Exposition. I enjoy thinking of their freedom. Properly to prize the blessings of rain, one needs to visit these rainless deserts. Bless God for seasonable showers! We are told that in July and August it rains so heavily here as to wash out these gutters we see along our track. But these desolate plains are said to be as fertile as were those in California, that with irrigation are now blooming as the garden of God and laden with the treasures of earth poured forth in response to the water of life freely supplied. So may our waste-places abound with the fruits of righteousness when supplied with the water of life everlasting.

The Southern Pacific follows a valley mid these arid hills in Western Texas that seems scooped out on purpose for travel and commerce. Very few human beings live on these plains. At long stretches there are desolate little groups of adobe dwellings with a grocery and post-office and that other great apparent neccessary accompaniment of civilization, "The Lone Star Saloon." Satan permits no opportunity to pass unimproved.

At Valentine, 1045 miles from New Orleans, the population is badly mixed, Spaniards, Frenchmen, Indians, Chinese, Mexicans, negroes, and American white men, all are seen as we pass by. The plains seem more barren than those already seen. Bones of animals lie bleaching in the sun. At Sierra Blanca I asked some Mexicans a question and they replied, "*No say.*" They were as dark as many Africans. I asked a lady there if they grew anything in that region. She replied, "Cactus only." Our railroad describes most decided lines of beauty as it curves along between these barren hills. The civil engineer must have had an interesting time trying to find a line for the track.

On a desolate spot on the side of a hillock was a small adobe about 8x10 feet, and in front was a washing hung out to dry, near which was a similar building placarded with "Room to Let."

A most careful company surely has this railroad in charge, for the track is fenced in for hundreds of miles where no quadruped large enough to be in the way of a train can exist. This is an example to other companies in lands where cattle live and roam. Here is an unbroken wire fence of 630 miles on both sides of the track from San Antonio to El Paso. When shall these deserts bloom? They were not made in vain. Before one hundred years have passed our population will crowd out here and some means of irrigation will be found, and these plains will furnish homes for American citizens. Fine opportunity is here opened to develop ingenuity and enterprise. Let young America try its head and hand and gain fame in blessing our country by extending the bounds of human habitation. Here is a village built of adobe dwellings. Fort Hancock is near by. Artists may here find something new with which to embellish an illustrated magazine. We are coming into a hotter clime and here houses have double roofs, the upper some twenty inches above the under to keep off the heat of the noonday sun. As we neared El Paso we gazed across the Rio Grande into the Republic of Mexico. On our side the river we found irrigation and luxuriant growth of wheat, alfalfa, peach trees, etc. El Paso is a typical city of some ten thousand inhabitants, I was told. It has a fine court-house, some good hotels, but there are many low, flat-roofed, one-storied buildings and many adobes on the out-skirts; good residences in the heart of the city.

About two miles west of El Paso we crossed the Rio Grande and were in New Mexico, which is desert indeed in that part. Drifting sands are a prominent feature, with sparse, stunted vegetation. Mountains appear in the distance. We turn our watches back two hours to keep company with the sun, which we have so far outrun. Here we met more Mexicans than any other nationality. This part of New Mexico is not very inviting—mountainous, sandy, arid. But we are told the soil is very fertile and, when irrigated, produces in abundance. Arizona presents the same general appearance as New Mexico, with like capacity for productiveness if irrigated. Surely, the water of life would be a benediction here. Traveling in this region becomes monotonous. Mountains and arid plains with cactus in stately loneliness, and small bunches of guyetta grass. I feel deep sympathy for those who traveled over these plains before the days of railroads. It is good for us that somebody lived and traveled and wrought before us. As we travel in Pullman palace cars, how little we know of the toil and weariness of those who came on horseback or drove teams. Good men and women, too, many of them were.

At Yuma, we find numerous Indians with faces painted and striped, and squaws arrayed in gorgeous robes. The men wear long hair, but no hats, in the hot sun. They have bows and arrows, and apples and oranges for sale. Yuma is a place of fifteen hundred people. The State prison is located here on the Colorado river, a strong, muddy stream, which we crossed into California. The same desolate appearance is presented still. Soon we pass through a valley, in some places 263 feet below sea level. In one locality pure, white salt lies like sand on the seashore. The railroad has a switch laid into it, and men are putting it on the cars for transportation. It is evidently the bed of a salt sea. Some day it may be a salt sea again. Desolation reigns supreme, and in summer it is said the heat is intense.

As we travel on, mountains grandly tower among the clouds in full view, and snow banks crown the peaks, the first snow I had seen for nine years. The chilly air gives us a cold greeting in this land of the setting sun. I put on my overcoat for the first time since leaving the sunny South. The mountains are utterly treeless, bleak and uninviting, many showing lava formation. They present a striking contrast to the Alleghenies in their utter want of vegetation.

At Colton we stopped off, and visited Riverside, California. Here we found the desert literally blooming with roses, and every tree beautiful to the eye, and fruits abounding in fine luxuriance. Wealth, ingenuity, skill and taste are here combined with labor and patient perseverance to render this place worthy of the reputation it enjoys. But more of this in a future letter. The picture now stands out, we trust, from the background, and we stop to look at it.

III.

We are told that the land of Riverside was as barren and the scene as desolate as much of that to-day along the line of the Southern Pacific Railroad in Western Texas and in Southern California. Irrigation and cultivation have changed the face of the country. Surely God put man into the garden to dress it and keep it. Though it produce thorns and thistles it may be made to bring forth much that is good. There is promise of better things to come. Beyond Riverside lies Pomona, in a beautiful valley, verdant in grass, shrubbery, fruit and ornamental trees and fields of grain. Roses bloom here in wondrous profusion and beauty. The mountains in this region are of great variety. Some stand off in solemn grandeur, wrapped in somber robes and wearing snowy crowns, hiding their modest faces in veils of cloud. Others, not so aspiring, are content with lowly heights, rise in gentle slopes, and are clad in garments of green to their summits. The vales between spread out in smiling beauty where living waters bless the land.

Soon we reach Los Angeles, a city of sixty thousand inhabitants, beautifully located on rolling ground, its streets lined with good business houses and residences, their yards delightfully decorated with a profusion of roses and geraniums of rare beauty. Fine churches bless the city, at whose altars minister faithful pastors, among whom we are glad to number our excellent Brother Chichester, greatly beloved by his people and consecrated to the cause of God, eminently blest in his work. Rev. Fay Mills was in the midst of precious meetings in that city when we were there. Surely God is with him. We greatly enjoyed his presentation of the good old gospel in an interesting way.

We received a royal welcome in this City of the Angels by dear friends of former years. Rev. Robert Boag and his estimable wife made our stay there most delightful. They live in a house embowered in roses. Nothing that kindness could dictate or thoughtfulness insure was left undone for our enjoyment. Sweet memories hallow our visit to that delightful city. Our friends took us out to Alhambra, a village of quiet beauty joined to Passadena, where all that money, taste, irrigation, mountain scenery, soil, agriculture and time can do to make a place attractive has been done, and has made this locality worthy of its reputation. The view from the grounds about the Raymond Hotel in Passadena deserves special mention. In Alhambra we met our good brother Rev. A. A. Dinsmore, who ministers to our church there. Here again friends seemed to vie with each other in acts of kindness and hospitality.

Leaving Los Angeles we went to San Francisco, where we met the same sort of reception we had in Los Angeles, and were taken to see the places of interest in that mistress of the Pacific which looks out through the Golden Gate to the far away Orient till the West fades into the distant East. We stood on Sutro Heights and looked out on the Pacific, and thought of some dear ones who had gone out through the Golden Gate to far-away lands to proclaim the gospel of our Lord. We thought, too, of Sir Francis Drake sailing by such a harbor as lay concealed beyond the narrow pass. Below us lay the sluggish seals, barking and twisting their lazy bodies. Then we strolled through the enchanting walks, grottos and bowers of Sutro Heights, mid evergreens, statuary and curiosities. The city park we found to be a place of wondrous beauty and loveliness, where for many hours one may wander admiring the combination of nature and art. In quiet nooks we escaped the chilly breeze which, in exposed places, detracts from the comfort of the visit. The ladies wore their heavy wraps and furs, and gentlemen their overcoats in May. They told us that ladies never wore light dresses in San Francisco, and that in summer they went off elsewhere to enjoy warm weather—that indeed their winters were milder than their summers. In Oakland, immediately across the bay, the temperature differs greatly from that of San Francisco. We attended the First and Calvary churches on Sabbath. We were told it was their time for the summer exodus, which accounted for the churches not being full.

We were greatly interested in visiting the Chinese Home for Girls. There were forty girls in the Home at the time. They sang gospel hymns, and did wonderfully well in reciting verses impromptu. Few of our sabbath-school children would equal them in appropriate selections in like circumstances. A young Chinaman, trained in the seminary of San Francisco, married one of these girls trained in this Home, and he is now in charge of a Chinese church there. The ladies have also a " house-to-house " female missionary. There is another school for Chinese of both sexes and various ages. This mission is greatly in need of a larger lot, a more commodious building and a more healthy location for this blessed work. Surely it is worthy of aid from good people everywhere. It is a privilege to help such a work, and train those who may return to bless the vast empire of China with the gospel.

IV.

San Francisco is a city of hills and cable cars, busy, bustling and chilly, but abounds in kind people. They told us their most disagreeable months were July and August, when the dust flies and the fog dampens it into paste on faces and clothing, when people find it convenient to take their vacation.

Taking the train for San Jose, we passed through a charmingly rolling country clothed in verdure. Fifty miles to the south we came to that city, in Santa Clara valley, one of the most lovely I have seen. The city is one of the oldest in the State, having been founded in 1777 by Spanish soldiers and their families. Including the immediate suburbs, it has now some twenty-eight thousand inhabitants. Forty trains daily pass in and out. The city is distinguished for its many handsome private residences and its costly and imposing public buildings. For its size and importance it is a remarkably quiet, pretty place, nicely kept. It has a charming park, and shade-trees everywhere; flowers on every hand, rare and luxuriant. The kind pastor of one of our churches there, Rev. J. W. Dinsmore, D.D., took charge of us, and one afternoon drove with us some ten miles by orchards of peaches, pears, almonds, cherries, plums, apples, apricots and oranges, and vineyards in abundance.

On the next forenoon he took us over the opposite side of the valley to the cañon in the mountain. The valley here is some seventeen miles in width. We drove perhaps fifteen miles by immense orchards of the varieties we saw the day before, only larger orchards; one contained three hundred acres. Grain fields and fine residences gave variety to the picture. From the mountain side we caught a glimpse of the glory of this empire. Twenty miles southeast of the city, 4443 feet above sea level, Mt. Hamilton proudly lifts its head. On its lofty summit the Lick Observatory is located, containing the largest telescope in the world. Like a faithful sentinel, the observatory eyes the stars in their courses, and has one of the grandest outlooks in all the world—over the Santa Clara valley, the glinting waters of the San Francisco Bay, and still beyond where heaven and earth and the Pacific Ocean blend. We called on that grand old man whose writings we have so long enjoyed, who is known as "Senex Smith," "Obadiah Old School," "Rusticus," and "C. E. B." We found him genial, jovial and hopeful in one of his orchards. Virgil under the spreading beech, or surrounded by his herds, was never so happy as he. In this valley of beauty and fruitfulness his fruits of goodness abound, and many call him blessed.

In driving to the mountain, we had a decided optical illusion. It surely looked as though we were driving on a down grade of at least five degrees, and yet the horse was stretching his tugs to draw our buggy, and a stream of water from the mountain was flowing in the direction opposite to that we were driving. The illusion was caused by the sight of the mountain we were facing. As we returned, we descended from the mountain in appearance as in reality.

On our return towards San Francisco we stopped off and visited the Leland Stanford University, and were charmingly shown the substantial, extensive and conveniently arranged buildings. The material is sand-stone in rustic dressing. The buildings are arranged in a quadrangle of Moorish architecture, generally one story in height, roofed with red tiles. A continuous colonnade connects all the buildings of the main quadrangle on the inner side, and surrounds a court adorned with native and exotic plants. The institution is non-sectarian, but under religious control, free to both sexes. As is well known, it is a monument to the only son of Senator and Mrs. Leland Stanford, who died in 1884.

The route on the Southern Pacific from San Francisco to Portland is full of interest. Mt. Chasta towers in full sight 14,444 feet in royal majesty, clad in robes of heaven's own purity, and dwelling sublimely beneath the stars. While traveling two hundred miles, we can feast our eyes occasionally on this object of attraction. Here nature revels in her wildest moods. Castle Crag and Sugar-Loaf stand in quiet grandeur, while the Sacramento tumbles over rocks near our track. The Black Buttes and snowless Sugar-Loaf stand out in contrast with Shasta, clothed in robes of ermine. A hot spring flows from near the top of Shasta. Wood is floated from mountain heights in water-chutes. There is good trout-fishing in the upper Sacramento river. The winding of our railroad is full of interest. It doubles on itself far worse than the letter S. The scenery is picturesque and exhilarating— snow-capped summits and verdure-clad mountains, valleys with streams and fountains. The day we passed through these scenes was perfect. At Sisson we stopped to view Mt. Shasta through a glass, fourteen miles away, eleven thousand feet above where we stood. At Mt. Shasta mineral springs the water spouts like a geyser some fifty feet in height, and falls in spray. The train stopped that the passengers might take a drink of the mineral waters.

V.

After traveling thirteen hundred miles in California we entered Oregon, and found it wild, mountainous, picturesque, with snow-capped peaks and green valleys and hillsides, sunshiny and delightful, much milder than in San Francisco. On Mt. Siskiyou I was reminded of Satan's offer of the kingdoms of this world and the glory of them, as they lay spread out in loveliness before us in smiling valleys, quiet villas, projecting cliffs, towering crags, romantic glens, mountains of God, monuments of infinite power, homes of peace, droves of beautiful horses, and a city amid the mountains. Here, at the city of Ashland, we stopped for a few minutes, and I met an old parishioner from Florida. We exchanged glad greetings and made a few inquiries, and we were hurried on. What a busy world! Scarce time to cultivate the sweet friendships of life. Here we can see only the beginnings, put some seeds into the soil and do a little cultivation. "What shall the harvest be?"

We rush on through a beautiful valley. Young orchards of pears are growing. Mountains in the distance border our valley. Yonder, twenty miles away, Mt. Pitt rears its head seven thousand feet towards heaven, clad in a hood of spotless white, which looks as if made in the clouds and fitted on by the angels. And here over against it are two gigantic fortifications thrown up by the Creator. They stand as if to defy each other to mortal combat. From the precipitous height of this table-rock, we are told, the soldiers drove the Indians over the edge into death below, and killed those who would not take the fearful leap We are now in the Rogue's River Valley, and will soon reach Grant's pass, so named from Gen. U. S. Grant, who was here in his young soldier days. Here the valley is narrow and clothed in green, and we glide on in comfort into wider vales of beauty and down the wondrous river, the Willamette, past those interesting falls which attract the attention of passengers. Soon we are in the city of Portland, and are met by our friends, who welcome us to this beautiful city of the Pacific coast.

Portland is said to be the most wealthy city in the United States in proportion to its size, having eighty-seven million-aires, one of the number being a forty-millionaire. It abounds in fine residences, surrounded by beautiful yards, carpeted in green, ornamented with tree and shrub and flower. The streets abound in shade trees. This city is located on the Willamette, twelve miles above its junction with the Columbia. The view from the heights in the rear of the city is extensive, and takes in the two rivers with their valleys. Portland is extending east beyond the Willamette towards the Columbia. It is five or six miles between the rivers at this point. Large vessels come up the Columbia and Willamette to the city of Portland. The Charleston and Baltimore of the U. S. Navy, were lying at anchor here when we reached the city. They attracted many visitors. They told us it had rained here constantly from November till in May, having cleared off the day before our arrival. We were kindly told we had brought sunshine with us. The soil seems so thoroughly soaked, it needs no more rain during summer, and vegetation makes luxuriant growth, and fruits and grains and vegetables are produced in great abundance.

This is a land of timber, too. Grand monarchs of the forest tower in majesty sublime. Fir trees grow so tall that a log 150 feet long can be cut from a tree. They are four or five feet in diameter. The forest composed of them presents a majestic appearance. I felt sorry to see good, straight, clear fir split into cord-wood and used as fuel. How different from California, where timber is scarce and fuel is high-priced. There they plant trees for fuel. This land was considered worthless, and Dr. Marcus Whitman found it very difficult to convince statesmen at Washington that the great far Northwest was worth keeping. They told him it was not worth paying taxes for. He had gone out to Walla-Walla Valley and found there was danger of our losing the whole of it. The Hudson Bay Company was planning to secure it for England. Dr. Whitman rode all the way from that far-away wilderness on horseback to induce our people to secure it. Surely our country is indebted to Home Missionaries more than can ever be repaid.

The General Assembly excursion on the 21st day of May, up the Columbia river to the Dalles, showed us scenes of wondrous beauty. One of our company, a physician, whose childhood home had been in the valley of Juniata, said to some of us that when a child, he thought the scenery on that beautiful river of the Keystone State was the finest in the world, till he saw that on the Hudson above New York. Then he yeided the palm to the Hudson. Now it is his deliberate judgment that the scenery on the Columbia as far transcends that of the Hudson as that of the Hudson transcends that of the Juniata.

The salmon fishery by means of great wheels is interesting. The size of the fish and the amount caught seemed almost incredible. I prefer not to give the figures given us and what we saw ourselves, lest it be thought I was telling a *fish* story.

VI

The picture of the city of Portland and its surroundings so impressed itself on us that we dwell on it with pleasure. The soil is good, and blue-grass and white and red clover carpet the floor of earth. Horse-chestnut, elm, locust and maple adorn the streets. The hills are so terraced as to form beautiful grounds about the homes of the people; cable cars ascend the steepest hills and electric cars traverse the city. From yonder heights we take in the city and the grand rivers beyond. Mt. Hood stands on guard clad in his robes of the snows of unnumbered years towering above the clouds. Mountain streams flow perpetually, pure and clear. They told us the weather was unusually fine while we were there. The people of Portland made us glad we had gone to see them ; they made us feel we were among friends. Day after day they announced in the General Assembly, that if anyone wished any change in his lodging place, or any change that would add to his comfort, please let them know and they would be glad to serve us. Their kind attention to the members of the Assembly we can not forget. Those people on the Pacific Coast have a freedom of manner and a hearty naturalness in greeting a stranger that has a charming fascination in it and makes one feel at ease. A man will leave his business and go with you quite a distance, if need be, to show you the way. Their hospitality and kindliness to us leave an aroma in memory that is delightful.

The General Assembly at Portland was properly called a " Pacific " Assembly. Kindness and good will gave character to it. There was a decided difference of opinion and of conscientious convictions on matters to be acted on, and there was a noble manliness in speaking and voting, yet a spirit of fraternity prevailed that gave every man credit for honesty of purpose in differing from another. I think there was not in all the speeches and remarks made so much as one sentence intended to hurt the feelings of any or to treat disrespectfully the views of those who differed from the speaker. The good Spirit of the Holy One was manifestly present in all our deliberations. The Assembly was especially blest in having a Moderator peculiarly endowed for the position. His quick discernment, sound judgment, generous nature, orthodox principles and genial disposition, eminently qualified him to preside in such an Assembly. His interpretations of the meaning of many points in our new book will doubtless stand as wise precedents for future Assemblies. I never saw an Assembly come nearer worshipping a Moderator than this Portland Assembly.

The representative character of the Assembly reminded one of the day of Pentecost where the people had come rom so many countries. In a little group I noticed men from Corea, China, India, Rome, Tennessee, Arizona, Michigan and Florida. Commissioners, corresponding members and others who had a right to the floor, numbered over six hundred. It was estimated there were at least one thousand visitors. When that beautiful church was packed full on the morning of May 19th, and the vast congregation rose and joined in singing " Praise God from whom all blessings flow," it seemed as though there were some of heaven begun on earth. The closing scenes of the Assembly were as near what such ought to be perhaps as they ever are in this sinful world. I trust the good Lord himself was pleased. I do think the Apostle John would have enjoyed it much had he been there. Then came the "good-byes," and we turned away glad and sorry—glad we had gone, and sorry we had to come away.

We spent a day in Portland after the Assembly was over and visited some kind friends we had not had time to visit while the Assembly was in session. Then on the second morning after the Assembly we left for Tacoma via the Northern Pacific Railroad. We had come via the Southern Pacific from New Orleans to Portland, and in leaving that road I feel I would not do my duty did I not commend that route to my friends. The "Sunset" and "Shasta" routes of the Southern Pacific I do heartily recommend. The appointments of the Company are good, and I was treated with kindness on the whole route. I was so comfortable that at the end of the four-thousand-miles' travel from home I was as vigorous as when I started. On June 2d we left Portland by rail and came down the valley of the Willamette and the Columbia, and were ferried over the latter river into Washington, and found the country largely a forest of fir, many of the trees tall, symmetrical, royal. We pass through some pretty valleys. The first city of importance we touch is Olympia, located on Puget Sound, over one hundred miles from the Pacific Ocean. Puget Sound is the Mediterranean of the Western continent. It is a study in itself. The largest ocean vessels can traverse this body of water in all of its wonderful ramifications, which afford ample, safe, unobstructed navigation. I know not its equal as a sound in all the world. They have over five hundred feet of water out in front of the wharf at Tacoma. Great populations, thriving cities, shall surely abound on the shores of this interesting inland sea. Tacoma and Seattle are two of them already well under way.

VII.

Tacoma is a city of some forty-seven thousand inhabitants, located on Puget Sound, built on a bluff perhaps three hundred feet high, beautiful for situation, on tide-water, the tide rising six feet at that point. This is a thrifty, growing, promising city, 102 miles from Victoria, on Vancouver Island. Tacoma is destined to be a large and important city by means of ocean-going vessels and through-railroads carrying men and merchandise to and from this far-away land. It is well supplied with saw-mills, in which we were much interested while watching them saw huge fir logs of perhaps five feet in diameter and forty feet in length. In "double quick time," with two immense circular saws, they cut a giant log into lumber. A stream of water in a chute carried off the saw-dust, and an endless band, with slats across, conveyed away the scraps, and supplied a fire which seemed continually burning to dispose of constant accumulations. This city has good, substantial business houses, and fine residences with beautiful grounds. It is a city set upon a hill, and of magnificent distances; has made an amazing growth in the past few years, and surely has a grand future. From the higher parts there is a fine outlook, the Olympian Mountains being on the one side, and the king of mountains, Tacoma, towering 14,444 feet towards the stars, clad in his robes of spotless white continually. With joy and pride the people of Tacoma point out this monarch of mountains to the visitor. He is a little shy, and frequently refuses to appear in his robes of state, and veils his glory from anxious eyes.

In Tacoma we spent delightful days with friends of former years, and were treated right royally. At church we met a number of Western Pennsylvanians, and felt quite at home. They are a sort of omnipresent race, and are found everywhere, and have the faculty of finding out good places. Western Pennsylvania is said to be not only a good place to live in, but a good place to move from. My observation has been that they are good material to build up new towns with, and other people are glad to have them. Our good brother, Rev. Jonathan Osmond, has a comfortable home here. Time has dealt kindly with him, and he is happy in the vigor of his years.

There is one remark I will make here that applies to all the cities of the Pacific coast. It is this: The conductors of electric and cable cars are, as a class, a remarkably fine-looking set of men, well developed, with intelligent faces, gentlemanly in their deportment, and much above the average in that employment East. I was told the explanation was that hosts of young men had gone West, many of them educated, some of them college graduates, and finding the positions generally filled, they had accepted any employment that was offered. I was impressed with this fact in Los Angeles, San Francisco, Portland, and also in this city.

Tacoma has a rival twenty-eight miles north on the Sound

Seattle has fifty thousand inhabitants, and is a much older place. It is situated on a hill which slopes gradually to the water, and presents an imposing appearance from the steamer as we come up to the harbor. In the rear of Seattle is Lake Washington, a fine body of fresh water, with a park on the edge of the lake, and cedar trees, said to be from eight to ten feet in diameter at the stump, and two hundred feet in height. The lake is fourteen feet above the Sound. A ship-canal from the Sound into the lake will enable ships troubled with barnacles to enter the fresh water, where they will soon be cleaned by simply standing in the fresh water. This I was told by one who claimed to know. It is proposed to make this canal in the near future.

From Seattle we sailed to Port Townsend, a United States port of entry, a place of importance as such. We met Mr. A. W. Bash, for many years collector of this port. He gave us much information concerning this region. President Harrison lodged with him when on a vacation trip up here. He pointed out to us the forest in which the President hunted wild animals. From Port Townsend we sailed across the strait Juan De Fuca to Victoria, on Vancouver Island. The island is four hundred miles long and one hundred and fifty miles wide, with snow-capped mountains, extensive coal fields, the largest on the Pacific coast, and furnishes lumber for export. Victoria is a city of ten thousand people, on the coast, with a good harbor for the largest vessels. It is a trade-centre for all that region; its gold mines on the island furnish now only about half a million dollars annually. It was the headquarters of the old Hudson Bay Company. Objects of interest there are the Esquimault harbor, British navy yard, government buildings, and Lord Dunsmore's castle. The climate is mild for so far north, but ladies dress in furs in June, and wear heavy dresses and coats, and gentlemen wear overcoats in summer. British sailors are seen everywhere in town. The place has a different appearance from an American town, but not antique, as Quebec. The streets are narrow and the buildings substantial. Electric street cars carry us where we wish to go, charging ten cents, Canadian money, for what our cars charge five cents. Immediately adjacent on the east of Vancouver Island are the islands, sixty in number, of the San Juan Archipelago, which once threatened to embroil two nations in war. Britain had possession on the north end of one of the islands and Uncle Sam had hold of the south end of the same island. A man cut down a tree half-way between, and it was asked who was entitled to the price of the tree. The question was referred to good old King William. After looking the matter over he drew a line on the west of the archipelago, and so decided it belonged to us. This is said to be one of the most interesting archipelagoes in the world, even to transcend in variety and enchantment the One Thousand Islands of the St. Lawrence. Old orchards abound on the islands.

VIII.

Our trip on Puget Sound on the beautiful steamer City of Kingston, from Tacoma to Victoria, was full of interest. The Sound, with its harbors and its channels, its cities and its adjacent forests of historic importance, kept us constantly on the lookout. Its indented coasts, deep waters, mild climate, and intensely patriotic people, brought in contact, as they are, with those of the Queen's dominion, we can not forget. We had the society of old friends, and of new ones whose acquaintance we had just made, so that June 3d was to us a red-letter day.

Victoria is nearly 49° north latitude, with the polar star well up towards the zenith. One is able to read by natural light at 10 o'clock at night in the long days of June. The heartiness of the greetings we received, and the friendly manners of those people of the Pacific coast, we can not forget. Pleasant memories come up as we think of them. As we look back on our mental picture of that Mediteranean of the North, with all that belongs to it, we are sure it will be the centre of a busy, earnest, active population, engaged in the varied industries of civilization, and conducting an ex‑ tensive commerce with the eastern continent, as well as with our own vast country and the British dominions.

The vastness of our country can not be grasped without traveling over it and stopping frequently to take it in. From the peninsula of South Florida on the southeast, to Puget Sound on the northwest, we have resources of such variety in climate and abundance in all natural supplies, and in all that is needed for the full development of a great and noble people, that if we fail it will not be the fault of our Creator, who has provided us richly with all material ready to hand. Surely everyone ought to be suited somewhere in our extended domain, and yet how many complain. A grander, nobler, more varied inheritance we can scarce conceive how our God could give us, far exceeding that granted to his chosen Israel. That was only a miniature type of this promised land reserved for us in this country of the setting sun beyond the western ocean, as the ancient called the watery waste beyond. What an incentive to secure this wondrous inheritance for Him who gave himself to redeem this world from sin!

On Tuesday night, at 11:45, we left Tacoma and crossed the Cascade Mountains. On the morning of the 8th of June, we bade good-bye to that king of mountains, Mt. Tacoma, as he stood in sacred robes of ermine, towering in the sunlight of heaven to lift our thoughts on high. We can scarcely wonder the ancients, without revelation, thought the mountain tops the abodes of the gods—so high, so commanding, so pure. The sight of such heights sublime has a hallowing influence on minds properly disposed. By and by we lose sight of that royal eminence and pass on through the valley to the Rockies. The plains in the valley are barren and monotonous. Small towns here and there, and streams from the mountains, occasionally break the monotony as we glide smoothly on. Some valleys off the through-line of the Northern Pacific Railroad are said to be exceedingly fertile. Walla Walla is one of them. It produces abundantly wheat, and fruits of many varieties. The city of Walla Walla, with seven thousand people and its institutions of learning, sits as a queen in the midst of the valley. Here it was that man of blessed memory, Dr. Marcus Whitman, first located as missionary to the Indians; he, with Spalding, introducing civilization and Christianity to that hitherto unknown region, and being instrumental in saving that empire of the great Northwest to the United States. This valley, blooming as the garden of God, is a fit remembrancer of the early labors of a Home Missionary in that distant western wild. The gavel of the Moderator of our late General Assembly was made of wood of an apple-tree planted by Dr. Whitman in 1838. The world moves, the cause of righteousness progresses, the land is being redeemed from savagery and sin; the completion of the good work is only a question of time. It is good to look back through long reaches, and see what progress has been made.

We pass on and enter the Rocky Mountains. Mountains, like men, greatly differ. Some are tall, some are low, some are bald, some well covered with natural growth, some wear an earth-grown head-dress, some are arrayed in those woven without seam in the loom of heaven, and these they have worn for centuries. Some mountains are gray and some are green, and yet are old. Some are well supplied with full pockets and are liberal in dealing out precious metals. Others are like ordinary mortals.

Here we are at Butte City, rich in mines of silver and copper. Its mountains are bald, their sides bored by prospectors. The city consists largely of plain, wooden houses. This is said to be one of the richest mining regions in the country. We pass so rapidly along through vast extent we scarce realize its magnitude. Since leaving Oregon we have traveled through Washington, an empire of itself, Idaho, and well into Montana, abounding in mountains, mines and fir trees. The plains east of the Cascades produce only sage brush. The western portion of the Rockies are something like the Olympians, clad in trees and verdure. The eastern Cascades and the Rockies on the "divide" about Butte are bald like the Southern Sierras of Southern California, Arizona, New Mexico and Western Texas, treeless, desolate, and grassless. But generally the Rocky Mountains have much of the beautiful as well as the grand, carpeted with grass, ornamented with firs, and alive with streams fed by melting snows on the mountain tops.

IX.

ROCKY MOUNTAINS.

As we glided smoothly on through a quiet valley in the great Rocky Mountains, looking out on their sublime heights and wondrous solitudes, and tumbling streams of limpid waters sparkling in the sunlight, we were reminded of that stanza of our childhood:

> " Morn amid the mountains,
> Lovely solitude ;
> Gushing streams and fountains
> Murmur ' God is good.' "

Waking from a good night's rest in our Pullman palace car, we were in fine condition to take in the grandeur of our surroundings. One pleasant thought insisted on being prominent in our musings. It was of the abundance of material the Creator had on hand when he formed these mountains. Towering in peaks and strewn profusely in lofty ranges they crowded thickly on every hand, and it seemed so easy for the Omnipotent to toss the plastic material into such fantastic shapes and inextricable confusion, yet with a certain orderly system apparent everywhere. We had been traveling amid mountains so long they seemed familiar friends ; yet we continued to climb till at last we were nearing the "grand divide" of the continent, from which the waters flow east through many rivulets and larger streams into the Missouri and on down the "Father of Waters" into the Gulf of Mexico. Those falling west of this water-shed contribute to the great Columbia which bears them on to the Pacific.

The Northern Pacific Railroad runs two loops or branches from Garrison to Logan. The northern loop leads through Helena, the other through Butte City. We do not know how grand the former is, but we enjoyed the scenery on the latter to the utmost of our capacity. The mountains here are rugged, bald, bold, picturesque, and well deserve the name of " Rockies." After leaving Butte City the sublimity of the mountains deserves special mention—rock piled upon rock all the way up, as we gazed on the heights above us built of Nature's solid masonry, till the clouds were left below, and, looking out on the other side of the train, it seemed rock all the way down—cañons and gulches vast, built of basaltic rock in Nature's careless, rugged architecture, not marred by any stiff rules, but easy, flowing, natural. From these towers of God much material, left over, lies tumbled about in Divine profusion in the shape of bowlders, countless as the grains of sand upon the ocean's shore. Yet these sacred places have been profaned, for on these wondrous bowlders we were compelled to read, "Southern Hotel. Meals twenty-five cents," and many similar notices, and this, too, in one of the most wild, picturesque points. Love of money! Enterprising Yankee! Is there no hallowed spot you dare not desecrate? I am heartily glad of that short sentence in the Book of God which reads, " Without are dogs." There is some place in God's dominions they can not invade who do not prize the sacred.

But here look from the car-windows! Above us, below us, and on every side of us tower mountain peaks in close proximity. Mighty, wondrous are the works of the Creator! We held our breath as our train passed over yawning chasms on slender-looking trestle-work. The rocky formations here are tilted sixty degrees or more, and giant pillars occasionally stand perpendicular. Ofttimes the rocks are built in solid mass for long distances and tower in majesty. Again, they are built as if by design in walls, and here they lie in careless style so closely, that the stunted fir tree has found no starting place. Wherever soil sufficient has been gained, the seed of the fir has lodged and the tree has reared its aspiring head. Here as we pass on we see the whole army of God drawn up, too vast to review. Mountain ranges tower in the distance and stretch in the blue atmosphere far away, determined to shut us in, while nearer peaks clad in fir, and broken by cañons and narrow vales, lie between. Mountains snow-capped; mountains without caps; mountains black and mountains blue; mountains green and mountains gray, attract our gaze on every hand. Mountains to the right, to the lett, behind, before, shut us in, and mountains beneath hold us aloft till heaven seems near. Tall, towering mounts stand as sentinels to guard these sacred grounds. Silence reigns in our car, for it seems that God is here ; some of us uncover our heads in his presence, and tears unbidden come. The very train moves slowly and reverently on amid these hallowed scenes. As we look, yonder mountain with a beauteous valley this side bursts with enchantment on our view to the right, and another peak and gorge on our left claim our unbounded admiration. Here the mountains are devoid of all vegetation except a sickly-looking grass which tries to grow on the detritus of rock, but does not make much of a success.

We now start on a down grade, for we've passed the crest of the Rockies. I confess to feelings of regret at coming down from those rare and sacred retreats. Gradually we wind down into the valley of the Gallatin river, one of the head waters of the Missouri. This valley is irrigated from mountain streams, so we see large droves of horses and cattle grazing in pasture-fields, and here are cultivated lands, with farm-houses and barns, presenting a thrifty, home-like appearance. Farmers are plowing, with four horses abreast drawing a gang-plow. Snow on the mountains makes the air chilly. A shower of rain is coming over the city of Bozeman as our train comes in. Bozeman is a candidate for the State capital. Flags are floating in the city in honor of the Democratic convention to nominate delegates to the National convention to meet in Chicago, June 21st.

Soon we reach Livingston, a rather pretty town in a valley in the mountains, where we spent the night, and next morning we took the train for the Yellowstone National Park. Our train leaves the main line of the Northern Pacific and at once enters the cañon and runs up beside a rapid stream, the Gardner river, between mountains towering in rugged sublimity. Through scenes of beauty and of grandeur we passed on to Cinnabar, so named from the red ore of quicksilver in mines near by. Here we took stage coaches for the Mammoth Hot Springs Hotel, where we must stop with our friends and begin to view the wonders of the Yellowstone Park.

X.

YELLOWSTONE PARK.

This park lies mainly in the northwestern corner of Wyoming, with a narrow slice only from Montana and Idaho. It is a rectangular plat of fifty-five miles east and west and sixty-five miles from north to south, containing about 3575 square miles, being about two hundred square miles larger than Rhode Island and Delaware combined. It is on top of the Rocky Mountains; the lowest elevation of any of its narrow valleys is six thousand feet above the sea, and several of them are said to be from one thousand to two thousand feet higher. Lofty mountain peaks rear their proud heads capped with snow, from ten thousand to twelve thousand feet above sea level, giving variety to the scenery.

In 1872 Congress "reserved this ground from settlement and set it apart as a public park for the benefit and enjoyment of the people." It is about the only way it can be profitably used. It is utterly unsuited to agriculture, and so volcanic in origin minerals are not sought for within its limits. Sheep or cattle would surely starve or freeze if they attempted to live there. But the Yellowstone is an interesting region to visit. We spent five days and a quarter in this wonderland.

We traveled through the park in stage coaches. We

entered it from Cinnabar and stopped at the Mammoth Hot Springs Hotel, where a good, lively fire in a large stove made us comfortable on the 10th of June. After lunch a company of us, with a guide to lead the way, made the tour of the Hot Springs, walking some three and a half miles up an ascent of seven hundred feet over terrace formations of wondrous beauty. At times we threaded our way through rills of hot water issuing from the depths. On the heights we looked down into deep caves bearing Satanic names. Some of our company descended into the dark abysses; some of us were satisfied with looking down into the caverns. We stood on the height, seven thousand feet above sea level, and gazed at Mt. Evarts, six hundred feet above us.

Next morning, June 11th, seven of us took a stage coach, drawn by four strong, reliable horses with a good driver. It is not safe to start with any other kind to travel up steep ascents and on the ragged edges of frightful precipices. We traveled forty-two miles that day through a snow-storm, over mountainous heights through an untamed country, by obsidian cliffs, boiling springs, steaming fountains, and by streams that in surging rapids plunged on to where they had a more peaceful flow. At times our roadway was exceedingly precipitous, winding around mountain peaks where gorges lay below, and at times up ascents where our noble horses would have to stop for a minute to blow and rest, before going on again to take us over the crests and down the other side.

Then our way led us through a narrow valley and by a boiling fountain; we soon, however, began to ascend again another hill covered with small fir trees. There is really no summer here. It may snow any month in the year. We were told that winter lasted every year for nine months and there was rough weather the other three.

At noon we stopped at Norris' Springs and took lunch and rested for an hour and a half in a large canvas tent, the hotel having been burned a short time before. It was cold and snowing, but we were so wrapped in great overcoats and shawls and blankets our intimate friends would scarce have recognized us. Again we went over mountain and by steaming fountain and stream and rugged highland, enjoying views that we were told by those who have been in the Alps, much resemble those of Switzerland. They who have been there say our own wonderland, in grandeur and sublimity, exceeds anything Europe can furnish.

At the end of an eight hours' stage ride we reached the "Lower Basin" and put up at the "Fountain Hotel"—a very extensive and comfortable lodging place. It is supplied with the modern conveniences—electric lights and steam-heaters, a spacious dining room, large sleeping apartments with heaters in them, and tables with a good bill of fare, all of which were prized by weary, hungry, chilly tourists. An extensive fire-place, all aglow with blazing fir five feet in length, gave us a welcome appreciated by our company. As soon as we had been assigned our rooms and thoroughly warmed and had eaten our dinner, we started for the geysers one quarter of a mile distant on an elevation in full sight.

We went direct to the most noted one in that basin—the "Fountain"—which was at the time preparing to give us an exhibition of its wondrous power. We stood by its basin and watched it boiling. As it did not seem quite ready for display, I walked a few rods further on where another geyser was at work. Looking about after I stopped, I saw I was standing about the centre of a square containing four geysers. One of them was named "Clep-Sydra" which seemed about as regular as a clock in throwing forth its boiling contents, shooting a volume of water scalding hot about twenty feet into the air, sometimes higher. The water that spouts from these geysers is clear as crystal, boiling, some of them, here on the mountain top, at 197° Fahrenheit and some at 188°. Repeatedly I put my fingers in to try it and jerked them back as if I had put my finger in the spout of a boiling tea-kettle. The force with which these streams of water were driven into the air was such that if confined an earthquake would inevitably follow. Presently another geyser near by, that had been fiercely boiling, was shooting its hot waters into the air, and its neighbor was in full sympathy and strove, if possible, to outdo its rival in tossing boiling waters.

Meantime I heard a call, and looking towards the "Fountain" geyser I had left, saw a dense cloud, and my friends were not in sight. I knew the "Fountain" was playing and started towards it. I found my traveling companions in full delight, looking on. It was shooting up a river of boiling water, some jets of which reached the height of fifty feet. The water falling back was dashed and churned till it seemed as if a terrific storm was raging, at whose grandeur we could gaze in perfect safety, standing a few feet away. This geyser has its regular appointment once in every five hours and fifteen minutes, and it is much more prompt in beginning service than many people. Its devotions last just half an hour and it quits accurately on time. It is surely faithful in rendering praise to the omnipotent Creator.

XI

YELLOWSTONE PARK.

I found it exceedingly interesting to wander all alone at "my own sweet will" over the vast mound covered with geyser formation, and hunt up geysers, large and small, and boilers here and there I had not seen or been told about. The Creator's law of "unity amid variety" finds beautiful illustration there. All sorts of figures and devices appear in the spouting of hot water from the depths. From the mighty "Fountain" already described, down to tiny geysers one-fourth of an inch in diameter, and some growlers, bitterly complaining because of their inability to send the waters above the surface and attract the gaze of the passers-by. Looking down the openings, I saw the water furiously boiling, and the steam issuing through the orifice. But they were only boilers, and could not aspire to be geysers, and so spend their days in unavailing growling. One can wander where he please, with care, and enjoy these ebullitions of power, seen in such variety, and of such character nowhere else on earth as far as reported.

I stood in wonder by the "Paint Pots," in a basin forty by sixty feet, with a rim from one to four feet high. This vast pot or cauldron is filled with a fine, white, pasty mass of silicious clay in constant agitation, bursting in bubbles with a flop-flop like boiling mush on an immense scale. Mud puffs send out spurts of mud, or paste, with steam, and this keeps up continuously day and night the year round, and has done so from time immemorial. After boiling for a long time, the white clay turns to a light pink. In the distance we saw steam slowly and constantly rising, indicating that this great basin on top of the Rockies was one of Nature's safety valves to prevent volcanic eruptions.

We were told the geysers in the park number seventy-five, and the boiling springs and paint pots between four hundred and five hundred. So there being more to see, we took our stage coach and traveled on ten miles to the Upper Geyser Basin. We got out at the hotel and inquired for "Old Faithful." "Yonder he is," said our guide, pointing to a mound eighty rods away—that is as near as a hotel is permitted to be to a geyser. "How soon will he play?" was our next question. "It will be nearly an hour, for he has just played," was the answer. As we stepped into the office of the hotel, we saw the "time-table" giving the times of "Old Faithful's" playing, as we have railroad time-tables. We soon walked over to the famous geyser. In playing for ages it had accumulated a mound thirteen feet in height, gradually sloping on all sides, by the deposit from the hot water spouted from below. The deposit consists chiefly of carbonate of lime.

While waiting for "Old Faithful" to complete preparations for exhibition, we wandered off to other geysers across the brook that flows near by. We kept our eye on our watch so as not to miss "Old Faithful's" playing. We returned when time was nearly up, and were ready, standing close by, when, true to his name, he gave us, on time, a magnificent display of his powers, and we stood and gazed for five minutes at the stream of hot water thrown with terrific force perpendicularly into the air from 110 to 150 feet high. There it stands, a column of water, constantly supplied and as constantly falling back outside of the column. It appears like a living thing of rare beauty and grandeur. In the sunshine it shows us diamonds of exquisite brilliancy and rainbows of celestial glory. We stood with feeling of unutterable awe and delight, looking at one of God's fountains playing for the enjoyment of his children. Surely our Father is pleased to have us enjoy such sights as lift our thoughts to him, and intimate to us how great and good he is, and what charming entertainments he can give in a world where sin mars nothing.

The waters of "Old Faithful" issue through an orifice, six feet long by two feet wide—its throat, into which we looked after it ceased to belch forth the hot stream at two hundred degrees Fahrenheit. If there be a breeze, one needs to observe the direction of it, and keep on the side the wind is from to escape being enveloped in steam and hot water. I was caught in that way the first time I approached the

"Fountain" geyser. I soon beat a retreat and was careful afterwards. We stood very close to "Old Faithful" during two exhibitions. A third time we stood three or four rods away. A fourth view I had all to myself some eighty rods distant, just before leaving this interesting locality. It was a parting salute I greatly prized.

"Old Faithful's" predecessor stands a few rods from him, with his mound as a great tomb with orifices yet, through which we distinctly heard his doleful bemoanings that he could be active no longer. In his days of active service doubtless the only visitors he had were wild animals of the lonely mountain heights—for methinks it was in the days before even the red men of the forest wandered there; and they are said to be exceedingly superstitious in regard to the geysers and will not approach them, declaring the Spirit of Evil presides over these amazing manifestations.

This Upper Geyser Basin has more geysers than any other locality in the park. They are named generally from some peculiarity in formation or of action. Some of the names are as follows: "The Constant," "The Twins," "The Triplets," "The Minute-man," "The Oblong," with four eruptions daily; "The Bee-hive," "The Sponge," "Castle," "Monarch," "Splendid," "Giant," "Giantess and Cubs," "Grotto," "Grand" and "Riverside." "The Chinaman" is a geyser playing from a great wash-bowl in which clothes can be washed.

One morning it was found that a chip had been taken from "The Sponge" geyser. On inquiry it was learned a man at the hotel had been up before day. His trunk was searched and the missing chip was found in it, and the man was taken in charge by the soldiers and marched out of the park at the point of the bayonet. The park is under military rule. Soldiers follow visitors, keeping in sight all the time when near beautiful "formations" to protect them from vandalism.

On our way back from the upper basin we got out of the stage coach to view again the "Excelsior" on the bank of Firehole river. Its basin is an immense pit of irregular outline, 350 x 200 feet, containing water of a deep blue tint, intensely agitated, all the time boiling, and with dense clouds of vapor arising from it. Its walls are perpendicular, cliff-like, overhanging on three sides, fifteen feet to the boiling water. We stood on its wall and gazed into the most horrid looking pit we had ever conceived possible on this earth. No wonder it is called "Hell's Half-Acre." For three years it boils and steams and seethes, and in the fourth year shows itself to be the most stupendous geyser in existence. Colonel Norris tells us he heard it spouting six miles distant. It causes the earth near by to tremble and rumble, and fills the valley with dense vapor. It throws rocks weighing a ton, and water in such quantities as to raise the river one foot in height where it is nearly one hundred yards wide. It sends away a torrent of foaming, steaming hot water and hurls rocks over surrounding acres. It is active for the greater part of every fourth year, giving two or more displays daily, sending forth a compact body of water from sixty to seventy-five feet in diameter. Here is a good-sized river shot straight into the air some three hundred feet in height. Niagara Falls is considered quite a sight. But there the river falls *down* 150 feet. Here it is shot *up* three hundred feet, boiling hot, with rocks thrown for variety. To stand, as we did, at the verge of this steaming lake, upon the hollow crust which projects over the boiling gulf, and peer down upon the agitated surface as clouds of scalding vapor arise, is awe-inspiring. When the geyser is in action, the terrific concussion produced by falling water, accompanied by rumblings like those of an earthquake, together with its disagreeable habit of vomiting rocks of various sizes, as if shot from an immense cannon, warns visitors it is safer to keep at a respectful distance during one of its exhibitions of terrific power.

XII.

SABBATH IN THE PARK.

Soon after entering Yellowstone Park we learned there was no arrangement for stopping over Sabbath. I went to the master of transportation and told him I did not wish to travel on the Sabbath. He replied that they had no Sabbath there, but if I would get up a stage-load of the same mind as myself, we could have command of the stage, and our stage could stop over Sabbath. I soon found a stage-load of my way of thinking, and on Saturday evening we put up at the Fountain hotel. On Sabbath morning I found quite a goodly number who revered the sacred day and were going to spend it quietly. Among them I found two physicians, Presbyterian elders, and their wives, from Western Pennsylvania, and several more from the same region; a Presbyterian minister and his wife from New York, and quite a number of others. One of the elders insisted that I must preach there that day. I insisted on the other minister preaching, but they overruled me. I then made inquiries for a place where we could assemble, and the use of the parlor was given us. I ask for a bible, and the hotel manager said they had none. I got one out of my satchel and inquired for a hymn-book, but none could be found. One of the ladies of our company agreed to assist in singing.

The soldiers of the camp nearby came in, dressed in their best suits of uniform. The hotel people came in, our tourists assembled, and we had a very interesting congregation. The ministerial brother from New York conducted the introductory services. We joined in singing the doxology, and after reading and prayer all engaged in singing " Nearer My God to Thee." Then for half an hour I preached to a most attentive audience. The surroundings were inspiring. We were on top of the Rocky Mountains, higher far than Moses was when on Sinai's top he received the law and communed with God. No human abode was near us. A little company there alone with God on the silent heights. God's wondrous power seemed visible in the rearing of those mountains and in the playing of those amazing fountains, almost in full view of where we were worshiping. The day was all we could ask. Bright sunshine was flooding the sacred scene. We felt that God was there. I announced a text and it preached itself. I felt I was only an instrument through which God was speaking to that little congregation. But rarely, if ever, have I enjoyed a service more in all my ministry. The audience seemed in full sympathy. The brother from New York followed with excellent remarks. After prayer we united in singing "Blest be the Tie that Binds."

It was a service we can never forget. They told us it was

a very unusual occurrence in that place. The soldiers seemed greatly to enjoy it. I had long, close religious conversations with some of them that evening. They seemed hungry for such interviews. Their religious privileges are very few indeed. Satan has his missionaries there. Intoxicating liquor, I was told, was secretly taken into the park, and other evil influences are there. I have no doubt but we had a much happier Sabbath at that quiet Fountain hotel than they had who left in stage coaches that morning to travel during the sacred hours. I was told of one gentleman who had control of a conveyance and had intended to stop over till Monday, but yielded to the persuasions of a lady in the company and went on. Some who observe the Lord's day at home seem to think the Fourth Commandment is not binding when they are on a journey. Some of Eve's daughters resemble their mother, and some of Adam's sons yield to their influence, and sin as did their first father. There is a growing tendency to desecrate the hallowed hours of God's precious day even among good people.

CAUSES OF THE GEYSERS.

I've been repeatedly asked for an explanation of the periodic geyser display. I will simply give that of Professor Bunsen, endorsed by Professor Tyndall and other eminent men of science. 1st. The presence of igneous rocks still retaining their heat far below the surface of the earth. 2d. Water (supplied mainly by snow and rain) having access to these heated rocks. 3d. Natural tubes by which the heated water may reach the surface of the earth. The tubes are filled with water from lateral drainage. The mountains there are on an average of seven thousand feet above sea-level; the igneous rocks are certainly as deep at least as sea-level, perhaps much deeper. The presure of a column of water in one of these tubes from which the geysers spout must be exceedingly great, putting the boiling point much above that at the surface. It can not boil, it can not create a geyser till the heat has reached a certain point. When that is reached there is a boiling-over—there is an explosion, and it continues till the heat is relieved and then it ceases till there is sufficient accumulation for another explosion. Such is Professor Bunsen's theory. It seems to explain the facts.

Before leaving the park we must take a look at the Grand Prismatic Spring or Pool whose dimensions are 350 feet by 250 feet. The water is of a deep blue, changing to green toward the edge. Gazing into this pool we saw the most beautiful prisms, apparently cubes of about one inch and a half in size, showing the colors of the rainbow, in a soft brilliancy that was charming. I felt chained to the spot, and I forced myself away only after all my traveling companions had gone. I feast on that picture yet and cannot forget it while memory lasts. It seems too beautiful for earth, and points perhaps to the better land where beauty reigns supreme.

It was with peculiar feelings our little company stood around the " Fountain " geyser the last evening before leaving, and for half an hour watched its resplendent playing in cloudless grandeur. It was calm, and the sunshine was warm enough to prevent the formation of mist. We approached very near the column of ascending water, and that one sight repaid us for all the visit to the park had cost us. I slept that night, June 13th, with a snow bank three feet deep just outside my bed room window, and outside the dining-room there was a pyramid of snow eight feet high. They told us the snow was five feet deep in the stage road to Yellowstone Lake, so they could not take us there. But we were not sorry for we saw lakes enough elsewhere.

We traveled in a stage-coach all day Tuesday till five o'clock, when we reached the Mammoth Hot Springs Hotel in good time to miss the stage going to the train. It had gone one hour before our arrival. We learned it was so ordered by the transportation company, as one of the tourists told us he tried to hire the driver to arrive in time, and he said the driver told him he should lose his place if he did. So we spent another day and paid $4 apiece for board and lodging. We wandered over the heights, examining the formation, and looking at beaver, bear, antelope, elk, porcupine, etc., caught in the park, to be sent on to Washington for exhibition. No shooting is permitted in the park. Brown bears come up in the forest near the hotel and eat food carried out for them.

I would advise my friends to visit the park the last of July or first of August, as at that time the snow may not be quite so deep on the mountain top. We headed a petition, prepared in a blank-book, to be signed by visitors, asking Congress to authorize the building of an electric railway through the park. Such a road would greatly facilitate travel, save labor, time and expense in the visit.

XIII

While we stand looking at these mountain tops and heights of grandeur, some one of a utilitarian cast of mind asks : What were they made for? Of what use are they? Well, their uses are various.

1st. They are sources of water supply. Yonder peak of everlasting snow, covered to depths that have never been measured—certainly a mile of frozen snow if perpendicularly measured at the melting line—forms a perpetual supply of water, a never-failing fountain, and at such heights tremendous hydrostatic pressure is furnished for natural hydraulics on a very extended scale. Through underground channels pure, cold, limpid waters flow for many hundreds of miles, and rush forth in powerful springs that never fail.

But for these mountain reservoirs Florida perhaps could not have her wonderful mammoth springs, that prove a very interesting study and are visited by thousands of tourists. One of these springs furnishes a stream so strong a steamboat goes on its waters up to the very fountain whence the river issues. This is only one of many wondrous springs, of such amazing volume as to prove the source must be some such abundant supply as we have described from those mountain tops. There are no mountains anywhere near Florida to furnish such a water supply. Chemists who have examined the waters of this peninsula say it is similar to that found in the Rocky Mountain region of the far-away northwest. It looks as though the southeast gets its water supply from the north-west. This great country seems mutually dependent, one part on the other.

2. These mountains are regulators of climate   They prevent stagnation in the atmosphere, and make North America very different from the continent of Africa, and from India south of the Himalayas, whose range runs chiefly east and west, and so cuts off the cooling winds from the north. Our mountain ranges, running north and south, are an incalculable blessing to our climate in the matter of health and comfort. The physical geography of a country has much to do with the character of its people.

3d. These mountains are vast treasuries of valuable minerals and precious metals, and furnish material for wealth that cannot be estimated.

4th. They are educators of the sublime. No one who has taken in those inspiring sights, that fill the soul with awe and bring him into touch with the great Invisible, can ever wholly forget them, or be just what he was before. Those peaks of grandeur, towering beneath the stars, are great object lessons of the all-wise, omnipotent Creator.

On Wednesday, June 15th, we took the stage-coach and rode eight miles to Cinnabar, at the gateway of the park, where we took the train and enjoyed the scenery of the cañon all the way to Livingstone. The Gardner River tumbles hurriedly down by our track to join the Yellowstone. Here, right by our train, towers a crag, on top of which an eagle has her nest. "The Devil's Slide," on the opposite side, rises in a regular slope to heights that would delight a vigorous youth to climb.

Soon we emerge from our cañon, and are on the main line of the Northern Pacific Railroad, 1048 miles from Portland and 1007 from St. Paul. The vastness of our country can not be taken in till we travel over it. Our Pullman car stood waiting for us on the side-track, and we were soon fast asleep. When we rose next morning we found ourselves still amid the mountains, with the Yellowstone flowing rapidly at our side. We followed its course for about 340 miles. At Glendive it left us to join the Missouri, and we felt we had parted with a familiar friend.

At Livingstone we had been told of immense bowlders, clinging by uncertain tenure to cliffs, at inaccessible heights overhanging the railroad track, liable to fall on us as we pass by. But the same kind Providence brought us safely all the way, and we came on, enjoying the scenery of that wild, romantic, historic region, past Park City, Pompey's Pillar and Custer, from whence the lamented general of that name took his last departure before meeting death by the Indians.

Sentinel Butte and Pyramid Park are most interesting ;

there nature revels in a magnificient park of pyramids of every variety. Some run up as needles, tall and slender; others stand as towers of regular geometrical contour. Some are after the pattern of the great Pyramid of Gezeh, in Egypt; others quite diminutive. Nature loves variety, and has shown her taste in this uninhabited city. These, as seen from the train, appear to be earthworks, having the appearance of water formation, well rounded, the line of beauty evidently being used in their construction. Nearly all these wonderful structures were painted in choice emerald, and the valleys between were neatly carpeted with the same. The picture was most beauteous to behold, all blended in perfect harmony. I would gladly have stopped off and wandered long in that secluded, lovely paradise.

Strange scenes of unusual beauty these, treeless but by no means unadorned. Picturesque they surely are. Memory loves to linger there. One might suppose these treeless stretches were sterile, but we were told that not even the valley of the Nile possessed such fertility. Like the rolling Pampas of South America, these prairies, carpeted with the most nutritious of native grasses, were, till lately, the home of the roving bison, as countless as the yellow daisies that nodded in the breeze.

Still on and on our faithful train steadily goes, by the headwaters of the Red River of the North and through the vast Dalrymple wheat farm, where farming is done on a scale of magnificence that excites admiration. Fargo and Bismark attracted attention. The huge steel bridge over the Missouri River, costing upward of a million dollars, is a fine piece of engineering skill. Remains of a pre-historic race are found on the high, rolling bluffs south of Mandan, on the west side of the river. On we go, till we find we are approaching St. Paul and Minneapolis, and a home-like feeling possesses us, as though we were coming back to where we had been before.

Then the good-byes began with our charming traveling companions. Some of us had been in company in the Pullman car since leaving Tacoma. We had occupied the same stage-coach in the Yellowstone Park, had stood together and gazed at the wondrous geysers, and were in sympathy with nature in her wildest moods. From the East and West, North and South, we had, in our pleasant car, compared notes and found much in taste and sympathy congenial. For our company to separate was akin to the parting of a pleasant family. The good-byes were warmly spoken, and many a kind wish expressed, and soon the twin cities were reached and we saw our friends of the Northern Pacific no more, but pleasant memories linger ever.

We crossed the Mississippi River immediately below the Falls of St. Anthony that were. They are now only rapids, sliding furiously down a great apron, placed under the waters of the river to keep them from wearing the bed of the stream from the height over which once they plunged. Grandeur has been sacrificed to utility. Water-power thus preserved is one of the chief sources of prosperity to the city. These twin giants of the North are vigorous in their youth, and buoyant with the hope of a noble manhood in the coming years.

Now, methinks, surely is one of the most desirable times to live of all periods of the world's history up to date. It is undoubtedly a time of grand opportunity. I'm glad I did not come into the world any earlier.

.

XIV.

While waiting for a short time at St. Paul, some one wishes to know in detail as to certain localities we've passed over. For instance, what is there in the scenery on the Columbia river that makes it charming ? Well, from the hurricane deck of our steamer, on excursion day, the panorama we took in included mountains standing as a wall, grouped in some localities like a vast amphitheatre. Soon the scenery changed, presenting pictures of romantic grandeur and wildness. Yonder a stream, from heights sublime, on the Columbia's banks, plunges perpendicularly down a distance of 850 feet, striking only once or twice while taking the fearful leap. And here in the foreground stand the " Pillars of Hercules," two immense columns of rock, hundreds of feet in height. Not far away, " Rooster Rock " rises out of the river. " Castle Rock " proudly rears its lofty head more than a thousand feet in stately grandeur. Cape Horn shows a menacing precipice abruptly ascending from the water, over two hundred feet above us. So passes the changing scene of terraced heights, abrupt cliffs, crags in curious shapes and mountain rising still above mountain, and over all towers Mt. Hood in serene majesty. But we must come on to other scenes, not so sublime yet no less interesting.

From the capital of Minnesota we traveled directly to the capital of Iowa, sitting right royally on the east and west banks of the Des Moines river. From afar you are attracted by the shining dome of the capitol, that crowns a massive building, well constructed after a model that charms and pleases, neatly finished, and surrounded by grounds laid out with taste and kept in good order. It stands aloft on Capitol Hill and commands a fine view of the city and country for many miles. In June the city was so embowered with foliage that it could be seen but in part. Good residences, with spacious grounds about them adorned with shrubs, trees and flowers, and carpeted with well-kept lawns, and fine long avenues running far out on gently sloping hills, make the city of Des Moines beautiful and desirable. The most complete system of electric cars traverses the city on both sides of the river, furnishing easy and rapid transit to every part. Tall, substantial, well-built business blocks occupy the central division of the city. Business activity was apparent everywhere. Some of these stately business houses now stand on lots formerly occupied by liquor saloons, and proclaim in language not to be misunderstood, that a city can prosper without the saloon. Nine years before, Des Moines had scarcely thirty thousand inhabitants, and abounded in licensed institutions for supplying the people with that which intoxicates. A distillery too was then deemed an auxiliary to the business prosperity of the city. But prohibition was declared to be the law of the State, the distillery and saloons disappeared, and the city has survived. The census in 1892 reports sixty-eight thousand inhabitants, more than twice the number that lived there nine years before, when the prohibitory law took affect. On Fair days, when crowds of people congregate, quietness, order and sobriety prevail, such as did not on like days when the saloon poisoned the atmosphere. Children of fathers, once drunkards, are no longer pointed at as drunkards' children, but are fed and clothed and sent to school. Boys are now comparatively free from temptation to the intoxicating cup. Though there may be some drinking on the sly, the prohibitory law is evidently as well maintained in that city as other good laws. Churches and educational institutions abound and prosper. We found our friends doing well there, contented and happy.

Another young city, forty-two miles further on to the southwest, has attractions for us and we pass on. Winterset, "the Gem of the Prairies," the county seat of Madison county, is a place we can not pass by. There we received a greeting such as few perhaps know except pastors who return after years of absence to a kind people with whom many years had been delightfully spent. Here language fails. To see the faces so familiar, and feel the hearty grasp of the hand, and look into the eyes of a host of those tested and known during years of pastoral service and familiarity in times of joy and sorrow, is a privilege above all estimate.

Twenty-two years ago I had taken charge of our church there, and for thirteen years had ministered to those people in sacred things. Many changes had taken place, but the body of the congregation remained as it was nine years before. A goodly number had gone—some to the better land. The marked changes were in the boys and girls and the trees. The boys and girls had come to be men and women, in whom, sometimes, we recognized only the eye of years ago. The body changes, but the soul that looks out through the eye remains essentially the same. Shall it not be so when we meet on the other shore and friends of here shall greet each other there? It was an ovation day by day while nearly a month of days passed quickly and delightfully away. It was a joy to preach again to those dear people. And how many social reunions in church and in homes and quiet talks in little nooks where scenes of other days passed in review!

The town is still in good condition. Many new residences had been erected, the streets were beautiful with overhanging shade-trees, and the yards with swards of green, variegated with flowers. The surrounding country was in its midsummer glory. When on top of the Rocky Mountains we longed for comfortable warmth a few days before. Now we reveled in the genial sunshine in a land of plenty, in homes of joy, with friends we knew full well.

To see the children of former years now active leaders in

church-work made our hearts throb more quickly, and we saw that the God of the covenant was true. Those dedicated to God in years gone by and taught the way of the Lord are now flourishing as palm-trees in the house of the Lord. 'Twas surely pleasant to review what God had done. But we had to say " Good-bye " and come away. We hope to meet again —meet ne'er to sever.

From Winterset and the capital of Iowa we came to the capital of Wisconsin, that sits so queenly between her lakes, beautiful for situation, the joy of the whole State. The central object is the capitol, standing proudly apart from the rest of the city, in a spacious campus of forest trees, on rising ground midway between Third and Fourth Lake. The streets radiate from the capitol. About one mile from the capitol stands the State University. The grounds are extensive and well cared for, and the buildings are numerous and appropriate to the purposes intended. The museum well repays a visit. You may linger long and be deeply interested. You will find the same to be true when you go to the Historical rooms of the capitol. Do not be in a hurry when you go, for you'll be sorry to tear yourself away.

We visited the city at the time of the annual assembly of the Chautauqua, and took it in quite satisfactorily. Many excellent lecturers were there and spoke to the edification of large and attentive audiences. I consider such assemblies fountains of blessing mentally, morally and religiously, as well as socially, under proper management, as I think they usually are. The day that drew the largest number of people, perhaps ten thousand, was devoted to the discussion of political issues by three prominent political speakers, representing three parties. The Chautauqua grounds are reached by crossing Third Lake in steam yachts. The grounds are exceedingly beautiful. Part of the time the weather was exceedingly hot and close, notwithstanding the lakes and prairies adjacent.

On the opposite side on Fourth Lake, on a retired bank rising gradually from the water, stands the State Asylum for Insane, which we visited. .The location, the grounds, the buildings and the management, impressed us as about as near what they ought to be as anything we expect to find in this sinful, imperfect world. Such Christian care for the unfortunate we find only in Christian countries.

We were told that with all these good things with which the city of Madison is blest, the influence of seventy-five saloons rests like a pall of evil on her. During the last quarter of a century we learned she had increased only three thousand in the number of her inhabitants, while ti.e capital of Iowa has increased nearly forty thousand, much more than doubled her population—this since she became a prohibition city. Is this chance, or is it in the line more or less of cause and effect?

XV

From the capital of Wisconsin and her lakes of beauty we had a charming ride across fertile prairies, yielding golden harvests, some sixty miles east to Delafield and Ottawa, where we received another welcome like that at Winterset. There we found a goodly number of parishioners of a quarter of a century ago, where we had spent some years in pastoral service, recuperating after seven years' pastorate in the city of Baltimore. There we were met by friends as true, with hearts as warm, as can be found in this world. These precious jewels, how we prize them! We think more highly of humanity when we find how good and pure and true many of the race of man really prove themselves to be. What cordial greetings! What kindness! How pleasant to recount scenes of days long gone by, and look into the eye beaming with goodness!

The years had made changes. The country was beautiful in former years, but more beautiful now. Villages and country homes had been built, shade trees had grown, and much adornment had been made. The whole community had become a favorite resort for summer visitors. One evil the good people complained of was the desecration of the sacred hours of the Sabbath by the great majority of those who come for recreation. It has a demoralizing effect on the residents. The tendency in many directions now is to banish the hallowing influence of God's holy day.

We could not stay long, so bidding good-bye to our friends we took the train and were soon brought from the quiet, peaceful homes of that lovely retreat to the bustling, busy, rushing metropolis that stands so proudly on the western shore of Lake Michican. The contrast was most striking. We could not but ask ourselves : What makes the people all wish to live so close together? There is plenty of room in our great country. Why insist on crowding, so as to destroy comfort, safety and health? "God made the country, man made the town." "God made man upright, but he has sought out many inventions." The invention of city building has its advantages, no doubt, but it surely has many evils. As far as the record goes, I believe it was the man that killed his brother that built the first city. I have wondered sometimes whether he would have gone into the business of building cities if he had not killed his brother. He seemed to feel very badly and be anxious for something to occupy his thoughts, so as to forget what he had done. Evidently he did not enjoy being alone in the quiet of the country with his own recollections, and seemed to be afraid somebody would kill him, so he wished to be within call of neighbors. He went out from the presence of the Lord, and there is no evidence that he ever built a church in his city.

Modern cities are much better, morally and religiously, than ancient cities, because of the influence of the gospel in them. The churches are fountains of blessing. But for them we doubt whether some of our cities would be much better than Sodom and Gomorrah. The ramified influence of the churches, with all that belongs to them and issues from them, so permeates the atmosphere of such a city as Chicago that their benediction cannot be estimated. This city, with its fourteen hundred thousand inhabitants, claims that the next decennial census will show New York to be the second city in size in the United States. Indeed there is no comfort now in driving through the crowded throughfares of this young Western giant. They say it is twenty-five miles from the north to the south boundary of the city. It seemed to take our train with locomotive about half an hour to come from the depot out to the limits where the houses were scarce. They boast of their twenty-storied building.

We sauntered through the Exposition grounds and viewed the buildings where the world is to show what it can do. I wonder if somebody will not be saying, "This is great Babylon that I have built!" If the sacredness of the Sabbath is to be ignored and liquor dealers have their way, I fear the result. "The heavens do rule" and God will not be mocked. "Whatsoever a" nation "soweth, that shall" it "also reap."

We had a delightful visit with kind friends in the city; also in that charming suburb, "Highland Park" on the bluff of Lake Michigan, a quiet resort where Chicago people have pleasant homes.

From Chicago we came to the "Queen City of the West," that peacefully rests on the northern bank of the Ohio. Coming into Cincinnati from Chicago seems like going from New York into Boston, or into Philadelphia as it was some years ago. There is some comfort in getting about cities of the latter class; one has time to stop and think, and not be carried along by the crowd. He can get a seat in an electric car and can ride without holding on for his life, as in Chicago cable cars sweeping round a corner.

Chicago's parks are places of enchanting loveliness, and so is "Eden Park" on Walnut Hills, Cincinnati. We spent delightful days with friends in the latter city, as we had done in Chicago.

A trip up the Miami valley showed us it had lost none of its beauty or fertility for which it was famous years ago. Middletown and Franklin have spread out and seem well-nigh like taking on city airs. Their paper mills have greatly multiplied and business prospers. Their churches have so grown as to demand new and more stately edifices. Lebanon moves on in the even tenor of her way, dignified, aristocratic, with educational attractions that draw hundreds of young people to her far-famed institution. Oxford, as of yore, stands a city on a hill, crowned with her university and seminaries, of which she is justly proud. Ohio is a grand old State, and the Miami valley is the garden of it.

Our visit to that region brought back days of former years, and memory was busy with associations most sacred. The tablets of memory have many records that are ineffaceable. How we love to read them! How interesting when the books shall be opened in the great hereafter! Nearly thirty-five years ago, in the days of our youthful ministry, we had charge of a church in this beautiful, fruitful valley. It was before the war. Times and homes and people have greatly changed since then. But few remain to whom we ministered there. To recall these scenes brings solemn thoughts to mind. Busy, happy years have passed 'tween then and now. We've no wish to live them over. A kind, gentle hand has led us, and we bless our Leader.

From Cincinnati we dropped south to Chattanooga, Tennessee, and spent ten days 'mid scenes of historic interest. On the crest of the "Missionary Ridge," a friend living there showed me in his yard a spot of mortal combat; two trees stand as sentinels to guard the sacred place where rest the bodies of some that fell there and were buried. Stone breast-works still remain as in the day of battle. I stood on a spot where two brave men in single contest met, and neither would yield till one fell mortally wounded. A soldier returned years afterwards and located the position where he was captured. His captor came at another time, and without knowing what the other had said, showed where he had taken his prisoner. Each told his story to my friend now living there.

As I was slowly walking over the battle-field, I saw two men who seemed to be looking for something. When I came up I found they were Confederate soldiers who had been in the battle. They were from a distance, and were now looking for relics on that interesting field. One of them asked if I could tell him where that house had stood a little below us, where the Federal sharpshooters were concealed and were picking off their gunners. He was one of the gunners. He went down and burned the house, and so dislodged the sharpshooters. Now he would like to find the location of the house. I did not find the place where the house he burned had stood, but I did ascertain where his battery was located and told him, which seemed to be a satisfaction to him.

XVI.

There are some localities that seem burdened with sacred memories, the mention of which starts a stream of thought freighted with treasure.

When a few years since we stood on the "Plains of Abraham" at Quebec, and walked around the monument of General Wolfe, on the spot where that noble man fell, memory was busy with the past. "I die content," said he, when he learned that the French were flying. As I thought of the results of the victory of that memorable day, giving vantage ground to protestants on this continent that has never been lost, I seemed to be standing on holy ground. I love to think of this mighty nation, which acts as a balance to the rest of the inhabited planet, coming on the stage on that eventful epoch. From that victory onward it was a possibility; a foothold and protection was secured for those who believed in freedom in the exercise of conscientious convictions.

Battle-fields, where earnest men with honest purposes contended unto death for principles that to them were more sacred than life, can not be uninteresting to thoughtful people. Such thoughts possessed me as I wandered over the fields of conflict about Chattanooga. One place of intense interest pointed out to us was General Grant's headquarters, from which he surveyed the situation and commanded the mighty forces under his control. One there can learn something of how much depends on the skillful locating of the different wings of an army, taking advantage of mountain and plain, ravine and river, day and night, and the proper moment of time to move. Over and through and behind all we can plainly see a superintending Providence, without whose ordering the best laid human plans utterly fail. The counsel of Ahithophel will surely be defeated if He who rules in righteousness so orders.

I spent days amid those historic scenes, thinking over the past and seeing, as I had not before, much as to how those contending forces were managed on those grounds now sacred to memory. "Chattanooga," "Chickamauga," "Missionary Ridge" and "Lookout Mountain" are suggestive names. On to Atlanta the armies marched and fiercely contended all about that city, making it historic. And "from Atlanta to the sea" Sherman led his men, the North knowing not where he was till the Confederacy was cut in two. Great principles were contended for and victory was slowly and surely coming. The final surrender was being made possible at Appomattox.

So methinks it is in the conflicts with moral forces and in the continuous struggle for God and the right. The true and the brave that fall in times of temporary defeat are to be honored equally with those who shall be present at the final victory, and those on guard or in out-of-the-way places who did faithful service and endured patiently and waited unrepiningly, without the inspiration of numbers, deserve recognition as well as those in more prominent positions. But for the former the latter could not have accomplished their mission. Each are only various parts of the one great army under the one Commander in the one grand cause of God.

We spent some time in wandering through that interesting city of the dead, the National Cemetery near Chattanooga. The grounds are surely of wondorous beauty and adaptability for the purpose. In a valley, accessible, yet sufficiently retired, gently rolling grounds nicely kept, there lie the remains of the mortal part of thousands of our country's defenders. A single white stone marks the graves of four thousand unknown soldiers. Here are memorials of a conflict that developed mutual self-respect in the practical acquaintance made in a terrible way. Each knows the other can not be trifled with, and perhaps we have learned enough of mutual forbearance and national patriotism to make our nation great and strong.

Yonder, towering as a sentinel of grandeur far above us, stands Lookout Mountain. It rises with precipitous sides some sixteen hundred feet above the Tennessee River, which sweeps in graceful curves through the plain at the base of the mountain. It well repays one to ascend that lofty peak. We took the cable car up the incline, and from our seat at the rear of the car we looked out at Missionary Ridge, which from the valley looked like quite a mountain. But as our car rose on the side of Lookout, the ridge gradually seemed to melt away and minify till it resembled a plain, and no longer obstructed our view. Soon we looked over and far beyond it and enjoyed a panorama that was certainly charming. We spent the day on the mountain top, from which we looked out on parts of seven States. Mountains and famous battle-fields, ridges and heights, valleys, plains, rivers, railroads and the abodes of men, contribute each their part to form a picture we shall carry with us while memory lasts. 'Twas not one of such awe-inspiring sublimity as from the top of the Rocky Mountains, but of soul-stirring beauty and scenery comparatively so near that one can take it in and quietly enjoy it.

At the Point Hotel we took the train and traveled round the summit. Our company stopped off and we wandered away into a lonely wild recess, where silence reigns and nature revels as she pleases, and we sat alone and thought and communed with Him who reared these lofty heights. We returned by the zigzag railway, which gave us great variety of scenery and more time to feast on it and digest it. When the government builds the boulevard along the side of Missionary Ridge and on through Chickamauga battle-field, connecting these many historic grounds, this region will be one of more than ordinary interest to thoughtful visitors.

Chattanooga has grown so that we could not recognize anything in the city we had seen nine years previous. In this place we have an illustration of what is meant by "the New South." It is an enterprising, wide-awake, go-ahead city. During the troubles with the miners loyalty to order was conspicuous. The citizens at once offered their services to maintain the law. There seems to be less of the spirit of anarchy in the South than in many parts of the North. I found business firms constituted of men from the North and South working harmoniously together. Half the extensive business men here, I was told, were from the North. The editor of the leading "morning paper" is a Northern man and was a Union soldier. Large numbers of Union soldiers were born and brought up here.

Two good drug-stores here are owned and managed by colored men. The colored people have a savings bank officered by themselves, and run successfully. They also have two or three church buildings nearly as fine as any in the city, and ten or twelve colored physicians, three or four of whom are educated men. They propose building an Opera House for themselves. They have three or four large brick school buildings. Hacks are owned and driven by colored men. They have a weekly newspaper of their own. They own a large number of residences and have houses to rent. They refuse to sell their property, and quite a number of their cottages are located on one of the best streets. A colored man owns and manages a coal business. Fully one-third of the population are colored. They have an Orphan Asylum for their children. Gradually they separated from the white people and are becoming more independent and self-sustaining. A colored drug-store has a colored physician, who sends out his prescriptions for colored people who patronize their own drug-store. They hold " Fairs," managed successfully by themselves. So they are learning to depend on themselves, and trying to rise by doing for themselves. The white people are disposed to give them a chance and to encourage them. The Southerners are greatly pleased at the progress of the colored race, and ready to help them. The colored people here prefer being by themselves, and do not wish to mingle socially with white people. In education, accumulation of property, and in business capacity, they are making decided progress. Their gravest defect, I was told, was in the line of chastity. In Chatta-nooga there seems to be no race quarrel; but they do quarrel among themselves. They greatly need the gospel in its purity and simplicity exemplified in daily life among their own people.

XVII.

From Chattanooga it is a pleasant ride to Atlanta, "The Gateway to the South," as it is called. Ten years had passed since we first visited Atlanta. Its transformation in those years has been amazing; there was scarcely anything we recognized as familiar. It impresses one as a beautiful new city full of vigor and enterprise, and exerts an influence for good on all the South. Beyond Atlanta we soon reach Macon, Ga., a somewhat typical city in the midst of an extensive cotton-growing district. By Way Cross we rush on till we cross the State line into Florida, which at our entrance does not present a very attractive appearance.

We are not long in reaching Jacksonville, called the "Gate City" of Florida. In former years tourists seemed to think they had taken in the State if they visited Jacksonville and made a trip up the St. John's River by steamer. That illusion has long since faded away. The glory of the Peninsular State is in its being in great part a peninsula. It lies four hundred miles North and South and juts out far into the Southern waters of the Atlantic Ocean and the Gulf of Mexico. There is no other peninsula on the globe as extensive and situated as it is, running far out from the body of the continent, cooled by the breezes that constantly play across it.

The different sections of the State are quite distinct in their characteristics. First comes the northern division, called North Florida, devoted chiefly to raising grain, grass and stock, and the cultivation of deciduous fruit trees, as pears, peaches, plums, figs, also grapes and berries. This section is not really on the peninsula, and is too cold for the successful cultivation of citrus fruits or tender plants of any kind. Next comes Middle Florida, where cotton and tobacco are extensively grown, and more or less oranges. It is sometimes called the Black Belt because so many colored people live there. Beyond this is South Florida, where the peninsula becomes in places only one hundred miles wide, and is called the Orange Belt, the natural home of the orange, where it is found in its native state, growing and fruiting without any care or cultivation. Semi-tropical plants abound in this section. It is this part of the State that has been settled largely within the last seventeen years.

Most of the northern people that have located in Florida have made homes for themselves in this southern division of the State, the true Peninsular Florida. The currents of air that flow so gently across this narrow strip of rolling land from the encircling Gulf stream bring balmy invigoration that is peculiarly delightful. The days are never suffocating, and the nights are charming. The breezes from the ocean impart a mild tonic that is exhilarating. The pine forests add to the healthfulness, and the sandy soil at once takes up the heavy rainfall, so that stagnant water in the rolling high pine lands of the interior is rarely if ever seen. The chief production of this portion of the State is the orange, where it grows in fine luxuriance and comes to a condition of perfection perhaps not attained in other lands. Vegetables are grown in immense quantities for the early northern markets. Many thousands of acres of orange groves, set out some years ago, are now coming into bearing, and good living prices are given for the golden fruit. As a consequence a feeling of encouragement and assurance is possessing the people, and many coming in from other parts of the country see how promising the prospects are, and are securing homes in this part of the State.

The churches are making progress here as never before. Good, neat, tasteful church buildings are going up, and manses, too, are being secured by the churches   Schools of a better grade are being established.

The Presbytery of South Florida extends from the Ocean to the Gulf, and embraces all the south end of the peninsula. Last fall we met on Indian River, on the Atlantic coast. Our spring meeting has just been held at Crystal River, a few miles from the Gulf.   These churches, planted and cared for now, will, we trust, in a few years, like the orange groves properly cared for, become self-sustaining and fountains of blessing in this fair, sunny land on which heaven has so richly showered its benedictions.

The south end of South Florida is a tropical land where the cocoanut, the pineapple and numerous other fruits grow in luxuriance south of the line of injurious frosts, in a land of perpetual summer. That region is now attracting many immigrants from northern regions of our vast country.

The rainy season in Florida comes in midsummer, and has much to do in modifying the heat. These brisk showers, coming daily for a time, cool off the atmosphere and impart a freshness that is most charming. This, taken with the fact that the sun rises later and sets earlier here than it does in the North, giving the land and water longer time to cool off and less time to warm up, has a decidedly modifying effect on the climate. The length of the summers produces a growth in vegetation that is wonderful to observe. Hence groves make amazingly rapid progress when well cared for. The dryness of the winters renders this climate specially good for invalids, and many come from the North.

The lake regions in the interior constitute an interesting feature. These lakes are fed from springs, invisible, supplying waters from beneath, clear, pure, soft, good for drinking purposes if need be. The large majority of these lakes have no connection with each other excepting the larger lakes. Many of the lakes are on the ridge running north and south through the central portion of the State, which furnishes the highest land in the State. Much of that land is high pine, sandy, rolling, with nothing to create disease.

Statistics prove it to be certainly one of the most healthful regions in all the United States. So low indeed was the death-rate that the Superintendent of the last census refused to accept the returns till they were verified by a number of witnesses whose testimony could not be doubted. These lakes, where they lie near each other, furnish protection from frost in time of a cold snap. Hence the southeast side of such bodies of water is considered a choice locality.

From Jacksonville we had a ride of one hundred and sixty-two miles south to Eustis, where we received such a welcome as made us glad we were at home again. With church, academy, public schools and friends, in the enjoyment of health, and plenty to do in the service of the good Lord, we surely are satisfied with the kind providence of our God about us.

Now we have gone across the continent and have come back by a different route. The picture of the many scenes of beauty on the way and of rare objects of interest, and the cordial greetings we received, stands out vividly before us and is a constant source of joy. If our readers have enjoyed the reading as we have the writing of these "Notes by the Way," I am satisfied.